TO THE BRAMBLE AND THE BRIAR

To the Bramble and the Briar

POEMS BY STEVE SCAFIDI

The University of Arkansas Press
Fayetteville
2013

ISBN-10: 1-55728-652-3
ISBN-13: 978-1-55728-652-9

18 17 16 15 14   5 4 3 2 1

Designed by Liz Lester

♾ The paper used in this publication meets the minimum requirements
of the American National Standard for Permanence of Paper
for Printed Library Materials Z39.48-1984.

Library of Congress Control Number: 2013953939

For Olivia Catherine, my niece.

For Dave Smith, my friend.

ACKNOWLEDGMENTS

Thanks to the journals and reviews in which some of these poems first appeared:

Shenandoah: "The Photograph," "The Bucket"

Blackbird: An Online Journal: "The Wine," "The Gentleman," "The Cavalry," "The Parade"

Poetry International: "The Cradle," "The Chickadee," "The Ship"

The Hopkins Review: "The Scythe"

Thank you to the National Portrait Gallery for their commission of "The Cemetery" (under the title "Portrait of Abraham Lincoln with Clouds for a Ceiling") for their collection, *Lines in Long Array: A Commemoration of the Civil War.*

Great thanks to Dave Smith, Ross Gay, Ilya Kaminsky, Chris Mazza, and R. T. Smith for their insight and encouragement of this book.

A special thanks to the poet Leslie Shiel whose generous patient reading over several years made this book a reality. Thanks also to Enid Shomer for her great kindness and her advice.

Thanks to Todd Hardy, Brian King, and Charles Lloyd without whom this book would not have been written.

CONTENTS

ONE

TWO

THREE

ONE

The Cradle   (Autumn 1901)

Kneeling down on the box, two plumbers cut a small
　　　square over where it was guessed the face looked out,
and the lead lining—soft for tools—cut easy

in 1901 when his coffin was opened the last time
　　　and seventeen men peered in to verify it was him—
Abraham Lincoln—lying so long dead inside.

They reported a yellow mold all over the black suit
　　　he had worn to his second inaugural. They reported
the small tuft of beard the coroner left prickly

on the president's chin after shaving his face in death.
　　　The flag buried with him was just dots and rags,
and a smell shot up to gag the children and the one

curious dog who stood nearby. They reported his face,
　　　a light green from the funeral powder, had turned
to lay sideways on the satin pillow. They reported

to Robert that it was his father and closed the thing
　　　for good, laying the box in a cage of steel onto which
was poured four hundred tons of concrete. However,

it was not reported that the sun burned like a mansion
　　　in the November sky, and that just before the workers
sealed the window, one reached a fingertip in to touch

the mole above the dead man's lip. He said it felt like
　　　the shock he got as a boy in a storm he thought was over.
Electric, but colder. A bee sting, burning ice and smolder.

The Boughs

Everyone was angry,
　　　mostly at the hurry

to decorate the house,
　　　to dress themselves

in black suits and colored
　　　gowns, and to make

a two-tiered cake of
　　　cornflower and honey,

and all the men carried
　　　the largest furniture

to other rooms and readied
　　　a carriage decked in

pine boughs, the odor
　　　of which intoxicated

the oldest, who were
　　　the most angry at

this impromptu wedding
　　　one step removed from

sin and the wrong of
　　　elopement. The ceremony

was brief, the minister
　　　and the groom laughing

nervously at one point
　　　in Ninian Edward's parlor

among the beautiful women
　　　assembled and the men

leaning against each other
　　　in happiness as the bride

entered slow and the lamps
　　　swooned from the breeze

falling in the windows.
　　　They received four chairs,

a platter, and an astral lamp
　　　that burned through

their marriage and long
　　　after his death and her

widowhood, the dual light
　　　of the lamps burning

a deep amber oil
　　　from the Indian Ocean,

which Melville helped
to gather years before,

climbing down into the skull
of the sperm whale with

a bucket and a rope tied
to his waist and a lamp

burning on his forehead
like the light of love itself

which Mary saw and Abraham
saw filling up the room.

The Cavalry

Under cover of the stars in July,
    a farmer arrived with seven
huge appaloosas snorting

on the lawn of the White House.
    One was wild, bucking against
the ropes and the wide net

pinning its wings down while
    Lincoln smiled marveling
at what some sugared oats

and Vermont grass had made
    of these horses leaping against
the bindings. Cavalry, cavalry,

said the man, imagine your new
    cavalry running through the sky.
Lincoln ran his hand along

the feathers stiff as shingles,
    soft as a lady's arm, and the man
motioned for him to climb on,

and when he was situated,
    holding tight, the farmer cut
loose the netting and watched

the president laugh as the creature
    bucked hard and jumped in the air.
The Department of War bought all

of the horses, which were shot from
    the sky one at a time over Sharpsburg,
falling into the houses like bombs.

The Palace

Sarah knew how to cipher
    and added up for her brother
his exact age when he asked.

Twelve years, three months,
    nineteen days. She gave him
her cakes. She pulled the fang

of a corn snake from the side
    of his foot. She hugged up
on him and said she loved him.

She could sew a pair of pants
    for the King of England if
she was given the cloth.

He wanted most of all to acquire
    for her such cloth. She liked
to follow, she said, the raw gold

of her thoughts. She kept a cricket
    in her pocket all one summer.
When she talked it was like a palace.

Often he saw his mother waving
    from the tower and smiling
he thought when his sister talked.

The Greeting

Something was said
    the moment after

their first meeting,
    and Lincoln turned

hard and shoved
    Frederick Douglass

against the stairs,
    and Mr. Douglass

punched him square
    on the nose, drawing

blood to shock
    the abolitionist whites

gossiping in the parlor
    as the men fell down

to the carpet rolling
    into a table breaking

two Hepplewhite chairs,
    pulling down the drapes

of sky-blue damask,
    letting light lurch in

as if drunk. The hostess
    took off her dress

and danced on the table.
    Dogs howled and sirens

began all over the country.
    It sounded like war

but it was only two
    Americans in agreement

mostly, crashing
    through the door.

The Telegraph

Not given to vulgarity or wild speech
  or damaging quicksilver
    changes of mood

usually, although in the telegraph office
  he swore and shouted to
    make the lilies

of the wallpaper turn brown and die,
  he sobbed and cried,
    he planned out

the murder of his generals or an efficient
  suicide, holding his head
    in his hands

like it belonged entirely to someone else
  and he was looking
    around for its owner.

Other times rare times he leapt up
  and banged against
    the chandelier or

crushed his hat with his fist for joy,
  but no matter what
    the circumstance

he walked home calmly like the father
  of a hundred thousand
    or two dead boys.

The Pot

The chair was a Windsor made of bent
yew-wood with a hole cut in the seat
     and a tin bowl beneath,
upon which the president sat to think

and stare out the window at the stunted
trunk of the Washington Monument
     and the barely finished
dome of the capitol and the wide open

spaces dotted with birds rising in stray
diagonals in the green sky of this day
     in which he will not die
or do much that is remembered. Pour

indigo ink into a small jar. Write telegrams.
Worry over shipping lanes and tariffs,
     the price of steel. For now
he sits on the Windsor pot and thinks

how soon the election will be lost and he
will return to Illinois to be lynched
     or not when the war is over
and the Confederacy elects Robert E. Lee

their new president who will send him
a telegram perhaps that says Abe, this is
     for the best. Lincoln sits and thinks,
a rash charging across his arms and neck.

The Tar

Before his mother
    pulled him away,
Tad saw the man
    being tied to a post

and covered in tar
    so hot it bubbled
in the pails, and he
    saw the rise of feathers

fall and stood among
    the crowd of white
men in Washington
    as the figure danced

like a rooster,
    and he never knew
what two boys
    beside him knew—

their father didn't
    dance and didn't sing.
He moved that way
    because it stings.

They knew what Tad
    did not but was coming to—
One day the world ends
    right in front of you.

The Well

Fallen into the well
in his backyard,
        he called

to Mary who
lowered a chair
        and a book

by a rope, and so
he passed a pleasant
        afternoon,

reading Shakespeare
out loud, saying
        a love song

to the circle of the sky.
The walls of the well
        long dry,

the words of the song
he memorized
        rang out

underground far away
from fortune
        or men's eyes.

It was early July
a Saturday, a high
        holy day.

The Beams

John Brown's body jerked around a lot,
     and he was inside there trying to fight
the indignity of his legs kicking up a storm

of laughter in the solemn minds of soldiers
     standing at attention, and his neck broke
eventually, lolling to and fro while his hips

worked like a dancer until it slowed, and music
     on the streets of Charles Town struck up
a sudden blast of brass and the streamers

flew and the drunks smiled into their sleeves
     and John Wilkes Booth cried tears of joy
for the death of tyrants, cheats, and traitors

and said his prayer aloud to the bosom of
     the whore who had her hand down there
for free, and the country rejoiced as the body

was stilled by its own force falling to nothing
     and was laid in the coffin and buried right
there where it remained lost for a short time

before it was moved to New York and myth,
     though it was just a body, the beard slick
with spit and mucus, the eyes spring loaded

to open, it seemed, though the captain tried
     to close them for they were hard and wild
to see—like two slender crimson laser beams.

The Dance

Known for his polite indirect way
    with the jury, he spoke slowly,

getting up to stand before them,
    this middle-aged, almost-old lawyer

apologized for the wrinkled
    suit and the ache in his back

and laid down on the floor of
    the courtroom, one at a time,

the flat worn soles of his shiny
    black shoes and won the day

for his client and made the judge
    smile while the lady stenographer

swayed slightly to the cadence
    of the slow proceedings as if

the courtroom was a ballroom
    in the back of her head and this

was a dance, which by a practiced
    lightness Mister Lincoln led.

The Hatchet

His sister was gaunt as a locust tree
    like his mother and him. Gaunt, lanky,
gnarled with dark hair, soft spoken
    and quick to laugh out loud, sounding
like a log splitting open, the interior

golden, shimmering hard as stone
    and good for every use under the sun,
which it resembles—the locust tree
    so bright inside. The wood was used
when his mother died and his sister

nine years after. The narrow coffins
    he helped assemble and to bury here
in the worm-tongued-descending-
    rung-by-rung offending muck from
which these fine trees sprung. *Death*

is all what living brung, his father
    said at the service. And every day after.
Lost and stunned from house to house,
    up and down the ladder rungs, Abraham
kills everyone in Indiana in his head

with a hatchet before the day is done.
    From the prairie grass north to
the bramble and the briar of home.
    Covered in blood, the boy inside
the boy begins while the hymns are sung.

The Kite

The traditions of springtime
    included the president
ringing a bell

on National Kite Day
    and a veil of lines
cross-hatching

the sky and four hundred
    figures running
in a blur

every which way
    along the South Lawn
above which

floated light machines
    of paper, ribbons,
and sticks.

So, hundreds of frail
    diamonds fluttered
in the sky

beside the burlap
    wings of an eagle,
or a horse made

of blue canvas and thread
      leaning into the wind,
and one ingenious

child, a girl of sixteen,
      lifted up inside
the bright swordfish

she made from woven
      willow sticks,
old lace, and straw,

disappearing slowly
      over the trees in the wind,
gone forever

from her owner who
      scratched his head,
watching it all as

the young lady turned
      the kite northward,
rising up toward

New York and Manitoba,
      sailing in a headwind
under the stars.

The Wine

As the bloom
    of the crocus

cuts the noose
    of winter away

so together
    in bed after

fighting hard
    in their usual

separate way,
    she lifts—

knowing he likes
    this—the red

wine-colored
    nipples

of her breasts
    one at a time

in the spinning
    house to

the dark slip
    of her mouth.

The Wheelbarrow

After his brother died
    and his mother
and his sister died
    and Edward his son,

he wondered
    about true north
and the fragile
    needle of a compass.

He wondered
    about daylilies
and the onion
    domes of churches

in the East. How
    could such forms
surge so gracefully
    out of the earth?

When dying is
    our direction,
how do we go on?
    He saw hydrangea

blossoms fountain
    upward like blue
waters in the yard
    of a neighbor.

He saw the long
       penis of a horse
swinging along
       lazily as it moved

down the street.
       He carried Robert—
his one boy—
       in a wheelbarrow

a while just to hear
       him laugh.
He was ready
       at any moment

to go. He could
       see underneath
every blessing
       was a shadow.

Two

The Chickadee

In 1857 Dred Scott was affirmed
　　a slave, not a citizen nor a man
but a thing like a stone or a bird
　　by the highest court in the land.
He woke and washed his face.
　　He rubbed his eyes with his hands.

His daughter Eliza gave him a kiss
　　on the cheek when she heard the news.
She gave him a pair of boots and
　　a walking stick cut from the vine
of a rose, that old symbol for love.
　　A few things useful to a man.

He walked out of the house to work
　　and rubbed his eyes with his hands.
The man who wrote the opinion of
　　the court, Justice Robert Tanney,
will soon hold a Bible, swearing in
　　Lincoln as the sixteenth president

of the United States and then he will
　　rub his eyes with his hands.
Soon Death will rise and bloom
　　inside thousands across the land.
For now it is quiet. A chickadee
　　sleeps in the gravedigger's hand.

The Hymn

The xylophone arrived accompanied
    by three brightly dressed ladies
anxious to dance and the ambassador
    from Istanbul, strangely aggressive

in his handshake and demeanor as if
    he were being forced to give up
an heirloom from his mother's side
    to whom he was closest, and when

the president smiled, the ambassador
    played and the ladies danced sideways
arm in arm with little baby steps,
    left and right, and the melody stayed

with the president like the xylophone,
    which he never played except to hammer
the random notes of his mood, long
    past midnight walking past the corridor

where it stood. Afterward, in 1865,
    the ambassador returned and played
for the stricken widow and her surviving
    boys the songs of his Ottoman youth

and "Green Sleeves" and finally "Nearer My
    God to Thee" and rolled the instrument
back down Massachusetts Avenue slowly
    to his parlor full of pillows in the embassy.

The Bucket

Shock at what he was. Shock
    at what he'd done. The man
all day was numb after this—

the unmitigated disaster at
    Bull Run. The dead everywhere
his own responsibility, the running

away a necessity for the Union
    because of his own amateur
performance as a commander.

He went to the barn to talk
    to his horse; he took an empty
feed bucket and placed it over

his head like a bell and sat there
    with his horse in the quiet
of his failure. The next day

his aides brought fifty books
    from the Library of Congress,
and he read each one aloud

from Machiavelli to the Iliad
    to the journals of Julius Caesar
and stabbed himself discreetly

marking an X on his chest
　　　to remember his shame bleeding
into his sleeves. Never again

would he leave the fighting and
　　　the dying to brave men, he thought,
I have murdered, such as these.

The Shark

The white man waved,
and the shark
    pulled him under

just off the beach road
in Maryland
    where the child

stood in a wagon
envious of
    the man rising up

again in silence,
blood bright
    on the teeth

of the fish rising up
to bring the man
    down again

deep into the cold
blue water.
    The owner

of Frederick Douglass
ran fast with
    the others to save him—

this anonymous dead
man whose leg
    they carried

like pink butcher meat
to the wagon
    where even it—

the leg—seemed more
than the minus
    of his own life,

his own mother gone
away, his own
    back raw as

the leg lying there
nearly naked
    turning blue

from the cold,
its new independence
    spooking the horses.

The Dish

Knowing hitahorfle
was the foreskin off
    an octopus dick

and guessing it was
the favorite dish
    of Abraham Lincoln,

Jeff Davis had one
procured off the coast
    of Alabama and sent

to the White House
on a platter with ripe
    apricots and a drizzle-

drip of molasses after
the second battle of
    Manassas with thanks

from a grateful nation
and a fork and a bib.
    Lincoln ate it standing

at his desk and said it
was delicious without
    a trace of bitterness.

It jiggled in the dish.
Of course, he said,
    I do love some hitahorfle.

The Puzzle

Home from Harvard,
    stretched out
bored on the sofa
    in the library,

Robert watches
    William walk
on his hands
    across the oval

room with a plate
    of figs balanced
on the soles of
    his feet as Tad

sings Dixie loud
    for laughs, working
a wooden puzzle
    of a horse

by the window
    while it rains
and suddenly
    everything stops—

William on one arm
    upside down leans
and Robert smiles
    with eyes open

between blinks
      and Tad sings
the last long
      syllable of

the word *away*—
      his mouth open
for the word *away*.
      Down south

in Hades they will
      remember how
their mother entered
      the room singing

along and ate a fig.
      How their father
followed dancing
      to the window like

he just won a prize.
      They will remember
this was the last
      best day of their lives.

The Coin

The only souvenir
    Robert clung to

was a copper penny
    from the first minting

in 1909 where his
    father's face gazed

in profile on one side—
    dark sheaves of wheat

on the other—which was
    presented to him by

President Taft one day
    on the rainy high

steps of the Treasury.
    Every morning the coin

was exchanged from
    watch pocket to watch

pocket as he fumbled
    into the day's new suit.

Sometimes in the middle
    of dinner, surrounded

by ambassadors and high
        ranking assistants to

the various deputies of
        the War Department,

he would reach quietly
        for the coin to graze

the outline of the face
        with his thumb. Sometimes

the difference between
        the official coin of the realm

and his father's scraggly
        black beard was too much,

and for days and weeks
        he would not look there,

although in loneliness four
        times he swallowed it,

passed it, found it, and
        placed it again into his pocket.

Once in Philadelphia he
        lost it and back-tracked

the streets until dawn
    with a lantern looking

down until he found it
    shining in the deep groove

between two cobble
    stones on Mercer Street.

He talked to it in the dark
    of February as if it could

understand his longing,
    and when Robert died,

this miniature portrait,
    worth so little, was tucked

into his hand. It was just
    enough to pay the man

who runs the rickety ferry
    that crosses the Potomac

twice a day even today
    to Arlington Cemetery.

The Jar

When the delegation
of western tribes
  entered his office

in their ceremonial
feathers and hides
  and pipes and sacred

dreams turning like
whirligigs inside them,
  Lincoln decided

not to tell a lie and
politely commanded
  each man to kneel,

and so their tongues
were then pulled
  out with pliers

and cut from their
skulls as they fought
  the soldiers, the chains,

and fires of the blade
and were sent away
  while the tongues were

collected in a jar
placed on his desk.
    He sometimes

swirled it absently,
the tongues dried out
    and curled. He

kept them soaking
in formaldehyde
    floating on his desk

for the rest of his life
as a sign of his
    truth telling and

the evil done by
even a simple lie:
    they were savages.

They were primitive
and dirty—like him.
    They were born to die.

The Torches

Concerning even the notion of the idea of one
    black soldier, Frederick Douglass
wrote seven terse elegant letters
    to the president.

Every day alone he visited with the secretary
    of war and whatever member of
Congress would listen to what
    he had to say.

He argued with the sycamores and the clouds.
    He could not convince anyone
of the power of a freed man
    with a gun or

the dignity of a uniform. Lincoln chewed
    on the fingernail of a thumb.
He was for this—and against,
    as the president

of a place lit with hate like torches in hay.
    Every day that winter it was cold
until suddenly it was warm,
    and regiment

after regiment formed and died and formed
    into ordinary lines of advance.
Each man with a rifle—objective
    as a scientist.

The Dollar

The Confederate note
  has the Arabic numeral 5
in the right-hand top corner,

the sallow nervous face
  of Jeff Davis below it,
the Richmond State House

in the center and the word
  Five spelled vertically
at the left. It could buy

a white woman for
  a day in New Orleans.
It could buy a wagon

ride to the auction house,
  this whip-ticket the rich
sniff and lick. It sticks

to his hand. He would
  burn it, but he likes it.
He would pantomime

wiping his ass with it
  for the cabinet. He will
die with it in his pocket.

The Cake

At the intersection of 12th street and New York
    Whitman carried a loaf of sourdough bread
under his arm like a newspaper and stopped

short, for coming the opposite direction without
    looking up was the actor John Booth practicing
his lines from Macbeth concerning the murder

of the king for tonight's capitol performance.
    And as the actor passed the star-struck poet
on the street, Abraham Lincoln crossed suddenly

toward them and briefly between them, mumbling
    his pardon as he brushed past them, returning
the last taffeta evening dress his wife would

ever buy with his money, the box like a five-tiered
    wedding cake obscuring him, so heavy and large
it pitched a little in front of him as he carried it

precariously there and passed between Mr. Booth
    and the poet, who both stopped together in the street
amazed to see such a thing—a huge white box

floating down the street with red raspberries
    on a vine painted around the sides and a long
silk ribbon fluttering in the breeze the box made

as the man moved down the street lurching a little,
    falling and catching himself in time turning
the multitudinous sea of the day incarnadine.

43

The Bride

Mary knew she was
   thought of as a shrew
a shrike a glutton
   a whore by half
the country at least,
   maybe more.

She knew her husband
   would come to wash
her legs in the tub
   if asked. Would buy
every silk dress
   ever made

if he could, would
   come to her room
every night to kiss
   at nine-thirty and then
at ten to undo her
   some more.

She was like a light
   to him. They were
their life. Two old
   friends who practiced
delight in the dark to
   the end.

The Robot

The inventor from New York arrived
    between the president's final angry
meeting with McClellan and an argument

with the secretary of war, and he was
    in no mood for foolishness and fancy,
so his astonishment at what he saw

purified something his burgeoning
    hopelessness was corrupting entirely,
and when the man made of metal and

rivets was led through the door by an arm
    like a bride marching awkwardly along,
the body shining at the welds, the broad

barrel chest gleaming like a silver drum
    and the bucket head so bright with sun
blazing, it blinded him with its high polish

of lustrous steel, he took the large hand
    and shook it firmly, coming to understand
thousands could be made to pick cotton,

to make shoes and fight the war. He saw
    the future is made of such things as invention
could dream of. He saw he would have to

rise from the dead one day and free them.
    The thing just stood there buzzing faintly,
looking and looking and looking at him.

The Swords

No one freed
    Harriet Tubman
from slavery,
    certainly not
Abraham Lincoln.

No one freed
    the man inside
a coffin traveling
    days in the bumpy
dark of a wagon.

No one freed
    the hunted
thousands from
    the belly of
the dragon or

broke its teeth
    to make a door,
no one except
    the people
the hunter was

searching for—
    the white hot
hate like a beast
    ascending from
the forest floor.

No one freed
     Harriet Tubman
but her own
     ingenuity and
her everyday

bravery, which
     was a sword
flashing most
     everywhere
as far as she could see.

The Parade

On the occasion of his nomination,

an eight-hour parade of citizens

marched past his house, and there

is a photograph of him standing

on his front steps towering over all

in a white suit with Mary in the far-

left lower window looking bored

at ladies in wagons with blossoms

in their hair, and fifty postmen

high-stepping in their blue canvas

uniforms marched along-side trappers,

farmers, and soldiers, and the lub-dub

of a tuba played for a hundred drunks

singing a hundred different melodies,

and donkeys brayed in the dusty street

and spotted calves yawned and dogs

walked on their hind legs balanced

on red-striped balls, and everyone

passed by his door it seemed so that

he understood America was stranger,

larger than even his wildest guess, which

already included multitudes almost

infinite as leaves of grass on the prairie,

all of them waving ready to be counted,

and one thousand was a boy carrying

a rooster under each arm, and five thousand

was a man six foot nine with a mighty

hammer in his left hand representing

the Carpenter's Guild in New York,

cakewalking as if through the pearly gates,

and finally beyond ten thousand came

a horse wearing a rig of wire and feathers

like a forlorn Pegasus walking slowly

as if exhausted, beaten down by the day,

and the nominee walked into the street

and guided the poor creature the rest

of the way through the city, talking quietly

of myth and the myriad varieties of hay.

THREE

The Pageant

The pallbearers
slipped skidded
   and dipped
in the mud toward
the tomb after
   the slow

train home, after
three days of
   rain, after
the final speech
   gave out
in the greening

valley, everyone
smeared with
   the murk
of springtime
in Illinois,
   and it looked

like a pageant
from a distance
   with a boat
drifting along
as the men
   in front fell

forward, going
to their knees
        then heaving
up again while
those in the back
        followed

back and forth
like the waves
        through a field,
the black clothes
of the mourners
        all dappled

like the horses
now standing by,
        watching
the procession
struggle, founder,
        and sink,

the spattered
coffin appearing
        as if brought up
from the earth
as it was
        lowered into it.

The Cemetery

He could feel his pinky toe
　　　push through the hole
in his sock, and a rash form
　　　on his neck.

He saw a hawk falling from
　　　a locust nearby, heard
a steam train cry far off.
　　　He smelled the citrus

perfumes of the dignitaries
　　　mixing with sweat.
Mostly though he listened
　　　and bowed.

Not far below him under-
　　　ground the leg bone of a boy
from Ohio, buckles, teeth,
　　　and rounds.

At the new cemetery
　　　in Pennsylvania he waited
to speak, the low clouds
　　　like the ceiling

of a church about to be
　　　torn down or replaced
with light, the crowd
　　　angry and somber,

slowly pressing in,
        the appointed speaker
talking too much
            of Rome on and on

beside the bones of
        the young laid down
before him. He sensed a hair
            on his tongue, fiddled

with his ear a moment,
        and then rose to speak
while the sky cleared
            and still continues

to clear—the blues
        of the sky a consecration,
a testimony for this
            new church founded

in Gettysburg, in hope
        and two hundred and seventy-
two words shouted
            over muddy earth.

The Continent

He remembers his lack of tears, digging
    the grave of his mother
        in the cold Indiana soil,

the ten year old and his father dug quietly
    while the white clouds huge
        and distinct as continents,

six of them, floated over his leather-
    bound book of geography
        at the edge of the dirt pile.

And the boy without tears told his father
    about Europe, Asia, South
        America, and the ice of

the Arctic and Antarctica and how
    Australia also floated just
        above these green pines.

And for such daydreaming he was
    smacked hard, and still the boy
        was surprised the next day

building his mother's coffin that the six
    clouds were still up there
        only now joined by

a seventh, which he told his father
is where his mother lives
meaning North America

and was surprised when the man held him
tight suddenly in the barn light,
holding his tall son

who never cried unlike him, who cried for
the first time in front of his boy,
who is now an old man

like thousands of old men all over America,
standing by a heap of dirt,
astonished by their hands.

The Dwarf

At the marriage of Tom Thumb
and Lavinia Warren,
the first lady wore a pink dress
to honor the bride

and to climb out of the earth
of her loss, and she
towered over the bride and groom
as everyone did,

even Tad who eyed Mister Thumb
with wary glee
and received a look one reserves
for a dog in the wrong

place about to pee, and no one
picked up the groom
like a Ming Vase and pranced
around the room

singing, although everyone
wanted to, even
the president, who was solemn and
respectful throughout

as was Mary, who smiled and
blushed, breathing in

the perfume of gardenias
and sticking her chest out.

You should have seen them,
she told her friends,
both so dignified and lovely,
both so fine and proud.

The Gentleman

Captain Harlan T. Nelson, stationed
at the White House as a guard,
    often saw the president talking

with a stray dog in his office or
as he walked to the War Department.
    Wandering through the house,

these lost souls roamed the halls
with their tongues lolling out or
    barking suddenly at the mirrors—

but one day late in September
a Scottish terrier click-
    clicked slowly into the office

and jumped onto the sofa
where Lincoln was studying maps,
    and the dog sat there scratching

at a flea and then said "I'm having
some problems with my health,"
    and Lincoln turned and

understood, being himself exhausted
to the bone, which the terrier
    sensed, and so they spoke awhile

of the cause of the Union
and the trouble with generals
    who will not fight and of the arc

and flight of hickory sticks
thrown, really heaved up into
    the blue sky so that it seems

they will never come down,
"Just floating" he said, "as if
    by magic." "Yes," said the other,

"the one thing that would redeem
everything else in life that is ruin
    and loss." "Yes, magic," he said,

"or love." Two sparrows flicked
fighting in the boxwood outside,
    making the branches spring,

and the gentleman suddenly
noticed the time, shook the hand
    he was offered, and wandered off

through the ornate hallways down
the front yard slowly toward
    the slaughterhouse and the wharf.

The Ship

Lincoln saw the banners
of the great ship
flashing in the wind
and the armada carrying
everyone black
back to Africa.

He saw them off at the dock
in Washington.
He dreamt of
the gratitude of everyone
waving to him,
the lonely Emancipator,

carrying through with what
he knew was best
for everyone.
As he told all of this
to the Black Delegation,
he was shocked to see

himself reflected in their eyes—
mirror upon mirror
in which two of him
stood hitting each other
with fish—like fools
in the sea. Two tall

white men convinced
drowning is swimming
and loss is lucky.
The Delegation listened politely
then told the president
about his country.

The Woods

He never knew who did it or why, never
could jog the image
    from his mind, two
        dead boys and a girl.

Three dead possums in baby-doll clothes
laid under the trees,
    each with a little blood
        at the mouth and nose.

He found them while walking with Sarah
in the woods on Sunday.
    It was something
        he never told anybody.

Three dead possums in baby-doll clothes
in the shade of a pine.
    Two in black suits.
        One in a little green gown,

their shoes tied with bows. The sleepers
lay in the shimmer-
    shade the wind made
        moving through the pines.

The mind can't move fast enough to get away.
So they ran and screamed
    into the fields flooded
        with light on a Sunday.

The Barber

From haircut to haircut,
        over the years his barber
slowly grew more blind

and more dangerous to
        the long looming ears
of the president who was

snipped here and there,
        drawing blood as Lincoln
quietly sat without flinching

to save the feelings
        of the one behind him
cutting away diagonals

and tangents of hair Mary
        would try to fix at night,
although in the morning

there he was—the man
        she loved, a dark shock
of flames sticking up

and the beard a shallow
        scorched ravine of bramble
and briar growing over bones.

The Photograph

Blasted with light for the portrait
    that will be engraved on the penny,
the lines of his face grow deeper

until he blinks and coughs a little
    and rubs his eyes afterward saying—
all right then now it is your turn—

so the photographer sets the powder
    and readies the camera for the amateur
who eyes him now through the lens

in the black of the hood—*now be still*
    Sir and take your medicine. Not wanting
to return yet to the war. More sitters

are found for the president, including
    a chimney sweep walking by and
a girl in a yellow dress with a bow

and then the two of us—reluctant to
    say no. Tomorrow six horses burn
in the stables of the White House.

The sound of their screams and the look
    in their eyes will stay in his mind for
another year or so. In eight minutes

in Cold Harbor 26,000 men will be lost.
    This man is the cause. He looks at us
appraisingly and then the flash goes off.

The Goblin

Ulysses S. Grant
was a butcher
    of young men,

thought Mary
who did not
    like his calm

demeanor, his
half-opened eyes,
    his gait like

a melody of
the darkest keys
    on the piano.

His cigar smoke
drifted everywhere—
    all through

her hair, her layers
of Chinese silk,
    her petticoats

and under-things.
Her own son Robert
    lived with him

now wherever
the killing was.
     Her little Robert,

his assistant.
The general talked
     a long time with

the president who
nearly worshipped
     the little goblin.

If these men
kill me anymore,
     she thought, I will

rip them from limb
to limb to limb
     and drink their blood

like wine. Like
wine, I will drink
     their blood like wine.

The Jellyfish

Lincoln's cabinet
sent a live man-of-war
    jellyfish, crimson

fringed and poisonous
in a glass coffin
    full of sea water

to Richmond. It was
summer again
    at wartime. The great

beast sloshed over
the countryside
    whipping its tentacles

in the box. When
Jefferson Davis
    had the lid pried off,

he saw the severed arm
of Stonewall Jackson
    half-consumed,

floating in the brine.
Of course it burned
    to reach in there.

A captain from Virginia
rushed in crazed,
    pulling on the arm

and died falling in.
It was awful. It was
    summer again at wartime.

The Button

Just after the Proclamation was law,
a lady traveled from the blue-top
mountains of Virginia walking

days all the way to the White House
and gave him a button from something
John Brown was hanged in years ago:

a leather chunk ripped and thrown
down to the dirt as the force of
the noose jerked his jacket open.

The lady-friend of a soldier kept
the secret token and passed it on
to another lady and so on to her,

this woman no longer enslaved, no
longer afraid, solemnly passing it on—
the object polished and prayed over

like a lover's golden locket, which
the man noted, holding it to the light
of the window where it gleamed.

He said his thanks and popped it
into his mouth suddenly coughing
and choking, working it slowly down.

The Tower

After Edward's death, she fell
    to her knees and remained

there for three days. After William
    died of typhus in the Green

Room, she called to him and called
    to him and called to him

and called to him and turned
    on the stairway when she saw

him disappear again. Every day
    Tad missed him. In March

Tad helped her find her poise,
    her sense of the windows

and the doors by stacking
    seven teacups and saucers

clinking in a tower on the loose
    bun of hair on top of her head,

guiding her downstairs,
    biting his lip to keep from

laughing at the rattle they made
    as they arrived in the kitchen.

He stood on top of the table
    and poured boiling water

into the highest cup with tea leaves
    swirling and sipped from it like

a gentleman come from heaven
    with tidings of her boys, and when

her smile turned to laughter,
    the crash of glassware caused

the president to rush in—in
    wonder at the sight like a man

covered with snow standing by
    the open door of a woodstove.

The Asteroid

The rumor was a tornado
sucked up a whole parade
    in Richmond—

all the floats, trumpeters,
and maidens and a million
    dazzling flecks

of confetti, but that was
months ago and already
    it is October,

growing colder and the sky
a deeper blue than the sea.
    Walking now

across the lawn of his house,
he hears the low tumbling
    blow of something

distant falling and looks
up to see a shining speck
    high as a hawk,

coming down, growing both
brighter and more huge,
    plummeting toward

him who moves just a step
closer to the great house
    while it crashes

to the ground, making a crater
and a sound like a body
    fallen to earth—

this tuba, come from high,
its wide brass bell crushed
    and ruined though

shining still, on which
the wind played Dixie
    slowly as it fell.

The Scythe

In the summer on Sunday
        afternoons
with a wire mask,
he would take his turn

checking on the bees
        and the honey
in the hive near the garden
of the White House.

Sometimes the gardener
        would quiet
the scythe to watch
the tall man in a black suit

looming over the bees,
        whispering
and coaxing, telling
them about the moon

and the Seven Seas.
        There was a calm
in his voice, a mysterious
something to which

many could relate.
        A timbre to the words

like a handshake
if it were spoken.

Slowly the bees will
        congregate.
His aide will traipse
through the shimmering

walls of heat opening
        the heavy doors
to fetch him a sweating
musical glass of ice water.

Soon he will lay across
        a stranger's bed
moaning, dying
bloody, and stunned.

For now though, a man
        kneels down
working in the sun—
his chest covered with bees.

"The Beams"
John Brown was hanged December 2, 1859.

"The Hatchet"
Lincoln's mother, Nancy, died of milk sickness in 1818, and his sister Sarah died giving birth when Abraham was nineteen. His brother Thomas died in infancy in 1816.

"The Wheelbarrow"
Edward Baker Lincoln (1846–1850) died of tuberculosis three weeks before his fourth birthday.

"The Chickadee"
Dred Scott (1799–1858) was enslaved until the last year of his life. He was survived by his wife Harriet Scott and their daughter Eliza.

"The Hymn"
In 1871, Thomas "Tad" Lincoln, died of tuberculosis.

William Lincoln (1850–1862) died of typhoid fever on a Sunday evening in March. He was eleven years old.

"The Puzzle"
Robert Lincoln served as the secretary of war under Presidents Garfield and Arthur. On May 30, 1922, he attended the dedication of the Lincoln Memorial. He died and was buried at Arlington Cemetery in 1926.

"The Torches"
Frederick Douglass lived and worked as a writer and speaker until dying of a heart attack in 1895.

"The Cemetery"
The Battle of Gettysburg took place over three days, July 1 through July 3, 1863. There were over fifty thousand casualties.

"The Tower"
Mary Lincoln died in 1882 and was buried in Illinois with her husband and three of her four sons.